WOW

If you were a

Palindrome

PEEP

by Michael Dahl
illustrated by Sara Gray

TOOT

PICTURE WINDOW BOOKS
Minneapolis, Minnesota

palindrome (pal-in) a word, a group of words, or a number that reads the same forward and backward

Editors: Christianne Jones and Dodie Marie Miller
Designer: Tracy Davies
Page Production: Lori Bye
Art Director: Nathan Gassman
The illustrations in this book were created with acrylics.

Picture Window Books
5115 Excelsior Boulevard
Suite 232
Minneapolis, MN 55416
877-845-8392
www.picturewindowbooks.com

Printed in the United States of America.

Library of Congress
Cataloging-in-Publication Data
Dahl, Michael.
If you were a palindrome / by Michael Dahl ;
illustrated by Sara Gray.
p. cm. — (Word fun)
Includes bibliographical references
and index.
ISBN-13: 978-1-4048-3162-9 (library binding)
ISBN-10: 1-4048-3162-2 (library binding)
ISBN-13: 978-1-4048-3573-3 (paperback)
ISBN-10: 1-4048-3573-3 (paperback)
1. Palindromes—Juvenile literature. I. Gray, Sara.
II. Title.
PN6371.5.D345 2007
793.734—dc22   2006027309

Looking for palindromes?

Watch for the **big,** colorful words in the example sentences.

Special thanks to our advisers for their expertise:

Rosemary G. Palmer, Ph.D., Department of Literacy
College of Education, Boise State University

Susan Kesselring, M.A., Literacy Educator
Rosemount—Apple Valley—Eagan (Minnesota) School District

IF YOU WERE A PALINDROME ...

or play many **SOLOS**.

If you were a palindrome, your letters would read the same forward and backward.

6

LEVEL

EYE

DEED

RADAR

If you were a palindrome, you could be a phrase or a single word.

A TOYOTA could break down at **NOON**.

If you were a palindrome, you could stretch into a full sentence. These sentences read the same forward and backward.

"WAS IT A CAT I SAW?"

If you were a palindrome,
you could be a name.

You could be a **MOM**,

a **DAD**,

mom

Dad

a sister named **HANNAH,** a cousin named **BOB,** or a **PUP.**

Hannah

BoB

PUP

13

If you were a palindrome, you could be a number.

If you were a palindrome, you could tell a short story.

SAVE THE WHALES!

SAVE THE WHALES!

"GO, DOG!"

?

16

ED IS ON NO SIDE.

If you were a palindrome, you could travel through history.

President Teddy Roosevelt thought a canal that stretched across the country of Panama would be a good idea.

A MAN, A PLAN, A CANAL: PANAMA.

If you were a palindrome, you could politely introduce yourself.

"MADAM, I'M ADAM."

You would always be the same,
forward or backward ...

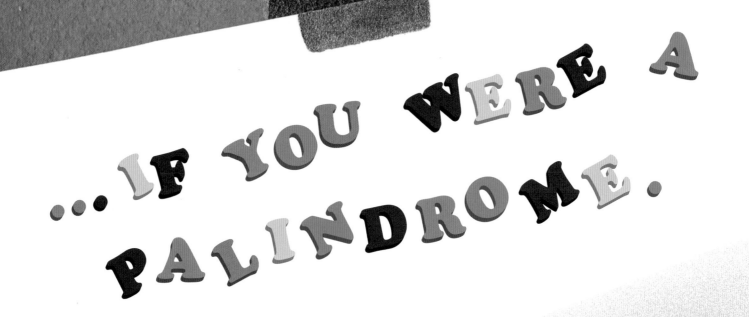

...IF YOU WERE A PALINDROME.

KAYAK BIB

RACE CAR NUN

Fun with Palindromes

Listed below are most of the palindromes used in this book.

Words

bib
Bob
Dad
deed
dud
eye
Hannah

kayak
level

Mom

noon
nun

peep
pup
race car
radar
solos
toot
wow

Sentences and Phrases

A man, a plan, a canal: Panama
A Toyota
Ed is on no side.
Go, dog!
I did, did I?
Madam, I'm Adam.
Now, I won!
Was it a cat I saw?

Can you think of other palindromes? On a sheet of paper, write down all of the palindromes you can think of.

Example: NAN entered a PULL-UP contest. ANA, SIS, and I hoped she would win the grand prize, a RACE CAR.

Fact: A palindrome is a word, verse, sentence, or number that reads the same forward as it does backward. *Palindrome* comes from the Greek word *palindromos*, which means "running back again."

Glossary

canal—a water passage dug across land for boats to travel through

palindrome—a word, a group of words, or a number that reads the same forward and backward

phrase—a group of words that expresses a thought but is not a complete sentence

To Learn More

At the Library

Agee, Jon. *Sit on a Potato Pan, Otis! More Palindromes.* New York: Farrar Straus Giroux, 1999.

Agee, Jon. *So Many Dynamos! And Other Palindromes.* New York: Farrar Straus Giroux, 1994.

Hansen, Craig. *Ana, Nab a Banana: A Book of Palindromes.* New York: Plume, 1995.

Irving, William. *If I Had a Hi-fi and Other Palindromes.* New York: Laurel, 1992.

On the Web

FactHound offers a safe, fun way to find Web sites related to this book. All of the sites on FactHound have been researched by our staff.

1. Visit www.facthound.com
2. Type in this special code: 1404831622
3. Click on the FETCH IT button.

Your trusty FactHound will fetch the best sites for you!

Index

Look for all of the books in the Word Fun series:

If You Were a Conjunction

If You Were a Homonym or a Homophone

If You Were a Noun

If You Were a Palindrome

If You Were a Preposition

If You Were a Pronoun

If You Were a Synonym

If You Were a Verb

If You Were an Adjective

If You Were an Adverb

If You Were an Antonym

If You Were an Interjection